The Threshold Cosmology

An Illustrated Philosophy of Emergence and Embodiment

GINGER DAUGHERTY

For those who have stood at the
edge with me—
and did not turn away.

For the edge.
And those who remain.

Acknowledgements

Born of listening,
where attention rests with what moves
before it is named.

Shaped in the unfolding:
in revision, in uncertainty,
in the discipline of remaining
present
at the edge of what had not yet
taken form.

I am deeply grateful to those who
stood near that edge with me—
who trusted what was still
becoming.
Your presence made this inquiry
possible.

To the voices across time whose
questions echo beneath these pages—
thank you for widening the doorway.

To those in my life whose courage
and becoming sharpened my own—
you are written here, even though
unnamed.

From that listening, a living
threshold unfolds—
not as conclusion,
but as practice.

May these pages meet you there.

The Threshold is not something
we create.
It is something we encounter.

Not as an idea,
but as a condition of being.

There are moments in human
experience
when what seemed separate
reveals relationship.

Where perception shifts—
not outward into something
new,
but inward
toward what has always been
present.

What appears here is not
constructed,
but recognized.

A pattern—
quiet, continuous—
emerging wherever experience
is allowed to unfold.

Across uncertainty,
transformation,
and return—
a continuity becomes visible.

Not imposed.
Not invented.
But inherent.

The Threshold is that
continuity
as it comes into view.

What follows is not meant to
instruct,
but to be encountered.

Not as abstraction,
but as experience.

And where it is recognized,
something in us
begins to align.

The Mermaid

Myth of the Deep

She Who Endures the Depth

The Mermaid

Raven-haired Mermaid
slipping through abandoned desire.

A delicate current
beneath the surface
of what was left behind.

Water rings gather
around her loneliness.

Languishing
within a circular mosaic—
a jeweled prison.

Glistening Black—
onyx mane and tail
shaped by rejection.

She Who Endures the Depth

There was a time when the air felt unreliable. Not gone—just out of reach.

She was living below the surface of herself, where sound travelled differently and light arrived fractured. Everything was leaning blue. Even hope had density.

Before she knew herself as something that could rise, she knew only immersion. The water did not welcome or reject her. It held her. It shaped her without asking permission.

She thought she was drowning.
She learned quickly that resistance did not preserve her. It exhausted her.
So, she stopped resisting.

She allowed herself to become fluent in submersion.
She learned the language of pressure, of suspension, of existing without surface.

She thought, "If I cannot reach the air yet, I will grow gills."
She adapted.

She became the Mermaid.
She Who Endures the Depth.

She discovered that survival is not always movement. Sometimes it is the refusal to abandon oneself while everything else dissolves.

She remained.
And because she remained, transformation became possible.

The Mermaid Becomes Air

She did not know, at first, that water was not her only element.
She believed herself made of depth.

Her hair carried the weight of abandonment. Her body drifted through corridors
of blue silence, where light arrived in fragments and loneliness circled her like a
slow, patient tide.

She did not fight.
She became fluent in suspension.
She learned how to exist without surface, how to move without direction, how to
listen to the language of absence. Rejection settled into her like onyx—
not as injury, but as weight. Something she could carry.

She became beautiful in the way creatures of the deep are beautiful. Untouched.
Unclaimed. Entirely her own.

Tiny prisms of light touched her skin. Bubbles clung to her, rising toward a place
she could not yet see. Her body responded before she understood why.

Even in the deepest water, the body remembers air.
It senses it before the mind permits it.
Before the heart trusts it.

She did not rise all at once.

Her circular prison was never locked. It was made of memory, of assumption, of
the quiet agreement to remain where she had been left.
When she released the agreement to remain submerged, the water did not resist
her.
It opened.

She moved slowly, intuitively, shedding nothing but the weight.
The blackness did not disappear.
She discovered that darkness could travel with her without defining
who she was.

When she reached the surface, there was no ceremony.
Only breath.

Her lungs remembered.
The air did not fault her for having lived in the water.
It received her as if she always belonged.

She was still the Black Mermaid.
She was something else as well.

Her body learned lightness. Her form learned lift.
What had once drifted began to hold sway.
What was once submerged began to listen from above and within.

She became fluent in threshold.

The darkness she carried no longer pulled her downward.
It gave her substance. It allowed her to return to the air
without losing the truth of where she had been.

The Black Mermaid did not leave the water behind.

She learned to enter it and rise again.
She became air without betraying depth.

And in that transformation discovered something more sacred than survival.
She discovered presence.
She discovered breath as belonging.
She discovered that she had never been meant to remain submersed.

She had only been learning how to carry the sea without drowning in it.

Psychological Translation—Immersion and Survival

The Mermaid represents the phase of transformation that occurs beneath
visibility.

It is the period when identity feels suspended. When language thins.
When what once felt stable becomes fluid.
This is not collapse.
It is submersion.

In this phase, the nervous system adapts to depth.
It conserves energy. It narrows focus.
It listens for currents rather than horizons.

Emotion is not decorative here. It is atmospheric.
The body may feel heavy. Time may feel altered.
Memory rises in fragments rather than sequence.

The Mermaid does not move quickly.
She endures.

Psychologically, this phase often appears as:
Withdrawal without disappearance.
Sensitivity without clarity.
Feeling without resolution.

The core tension is this:
How to remain intact while immersed.
The impulse may be to surface immediately—
to explain, to solve, to escape intensity.

But depth has its own intelligence.
Water does not move in straight lines.
It surrounds. It absorbs. It presses inward
until something unnecessary loosens.

The Mermaid phase refines emotional capacity.
It teaches tolerance for ambiguity.
It strengthens the ability to feel
without fragmenting.
It widens the container of the heart.

Survival here is not dramatic.
It is rhythmic.

Breath held.
Breath released.
Breath held again.

Over time, what once felt overwhelming becomes navigable.
Emotion becomes information rather than threat.
Depth becomes wisdom rather than danger.

In the cosmology,
Water is the beginning because it strips away performance.

Before boundary.
Before expansion.
Before embodiment.
There is immersion.

And in immersion, something essential remains.

The Mermaid does not teach escape from feeling.
She teaches how to live within it without dissolving.

Edges softened into current

Stay

Breathe beneath it

The Raven

Myth of Unmasking

She Who Swallowed the False Sun

The Raven

Raven rids herself
of predators.

She makes way for beauty.
Never second-guesses.

She knows
there is logic in empathy.

Though pain-stricken,
eternally black—
she is not haunted,
but remembering.

What devours
is devoured.

Darkness remains—
but does not claim her.

She is the Raven—
descending.

She Who Swallowed the False Sun

Before she knew herself as winged, she had openness.
She did not yet have feathers. She had awareness.

She lived without boundary listening to all that moved through the field around her. She felt beauty and distortion the same. She did not yet know how to distinguish what belonged to her and what had trespassed.

She believed her openness was strength. And it was. But it left her permeable.

She watched carefully, learning the shapes of threat, the patterns of harm, the quiet logic of survival. She learned that predators do not always arrive as violence. Sometimes they arrive as certainty. Sometimes they enter what is open naming it as their own. They cast false light without warmth, leaving behind shadows.

She carried many shadows. She believed they were hers.

And for a time, she stood beneath that false sun—the light that does not illuminate, but distorts—motionless.
She believed she was the distortion.

Until the moment when endurance was no longer enough and something older than fear awakened. It was not anger. It was recognition.

She saw with sudden clarity that what she carried inside, had not been born from her. The shadows were real, but their authority was not.

She understood then that openness without boundary is not compassion. It is erasure.

She swallowed the false sun whole.
Not to destroy it, but to remove its authority.

The shadows settled into her bones as structure. They became density without distortion. They became boundary.

Her spine lengthened. Her bones grew lighter. Her breath deepened. Something ancient began to unfold within—not imposed, but remembered.

Feathers emerged where endurance had been. Wings formed not for escape, but for continuation.

She did not open them immediately. She stood at the threshold between ground and sky, listening.
The air had not yet claimed her.

She extended her wings slowly, feeling their weight, their reach, their truth as part of her. The air now moved across them as if it had been waiting.
When she opened them fully it was not dramatic. It was sovereignty. She did not rise to escape what she had been. She rose because she could now carry it without collapse.

She learned that flight is not the absence of gravity. It is the relationship to it. She became the keeper of that relationship.

She did not remove shadow from herself. She integrated it so completely that it could no longer rule her.

She did not close herself to the world. She refined her openness into discernment. She positioned herself at the threshold—not to block passage, but to preserve integrity.

Her wings do not open for show. They open when truth requires protection and when boundary must be remembered.

She became the Raven.
Guardian of Boundary and Truth.

When the Raven First Opened Her Wings

Before she opened her wings, she knew gravity more intimately than air.
She lived close to the ground, where sound fell heavily and silence carried weight.

Nothing in her world promised lift.
There was only endurance—
The art of remaining intact while unseen forces pressed inward,
shaping her shadow.

She watched.
Not with fear—
with stillness.

She learned the tremor in the air before a storm arrived.
She felt the shift in the temperature when hunger entered a room.
She knew the difference between noise and truth.

The change began in secret.
Her bones thinned like winter
branches.
Her breath moved lower,
then wider,
as if space inside her
had quietly increased.
Along her back something gathered.
Not pain.
Pressure becoming form.

There comes a moment
when remaining small
weighs more than unfolding.
She reached it without witness.
No command.
No revelation.
Only widening.

She did not reach upward.
She opened.

What had slept folded within unfurled—
dark and deliberate.
Feathers emerged
like ink against sky,
each one marked
with nights endured,
truth held,
boundaries drawn without speech.

Her wings were not for decoration.
They were for weather.
She held them open
without moving.

The air moved first.
It passed across her span
as if remembering her shape.

It began in listening.

She stood between earth and sky,
belonging to both and neither.
The ground still claimed her weight.
The sky did not yet hold her.

She did not leap.
She measured stroke.
A shift in balance.

Gravity did not release her.
It answered.
Lift was not escape.
It was accord.

Below her,
the earth remained dark and
constant.
Above her,
The sky remained wide and
unpromised.
She moved between them.

This was her first knowing:
She was not meant for one element.
She was threshold made flesh.
She could descend without
drowning shadow.
She could rise without abandoning
the ground.
She could cross the unseen line
and remain herself.

Her wings did not make her new.
They made her visible to herself.

And when she folded them again,
the dark did not swallow her.
It settled around her
like a rightful night.

For once a wing has opened in truth,
it does not close in fear.
It closes in sovereignty.

Psychological Translation—Discernment and Sovereignty

The Raven represents the phase of transformation in which perception sharpens.

After immersion, something begins to clarify.
What was once felt becomes named.
What was endured becomes understood.

This is the stage of differentiation.
The nervous system, having adapted to depth, begins to reorganize around structure.

The body learns the difference between:
Threat and memory.
Noise and signal.
Presence and intrusion.

Where the Mermaid tolerated intensity,
the Raven defines its limits.

This phase is marked by posture.
The spine lengthens.
The gaze steadies.
The breath becomes more
directional.

Psychologically, this appears as:
A refusal to absorb what does not belong.
A willingness to confront internal contradiction.
A capacity to say no without collapse.

The core tension here is not survival.
It is clarity.
Clarity can feel sharp at first.
It may cut away relationships, identities, or beliefs that once provided safety.

The Raven does not reject shadow.
She studies it.
She integrates what is true and releases what is distortion.

Boundary, in this phase, is not aggression.
It is contour.
Without contour, depth floods everything.
Without discernment, expansion becomes chaotic.

The Raven phase establishes internal sovereignty.
The individual no longer organizes around reaction.
They organize around principle.
This is not rigidity.
It is alignment.

The body reflects this change.
Energy is no longer scattered.
Attention is no longer diffused.
Movement becomes intentional.

In the cosmology, Shadow is not darkness to be eliminated.
It is contrast that defines shape.

The Raven teaches that truth is not always gentle.
But it is stabilizing.
Without her, expansion would have no spine.

She marks the threshold between immersion and movement.
She guards the interval where identity reforms.

And once perception has sharpened,
what rises next can do so without fragmentation.

Stand

What is true remains

The Dragonfly

Myth of the Threshold

She Who Lives Between Worlds

The Dragonfly

Soaring,
I glitter—
longing for home.

Knowing,
I shall not stay
for long.

Rooted to solitude—
circles intrinsic to strength.

Subject to wind
and rain.

With fragile, lacey wings—
and a fierce, stubborn jaw.

Awkward on earth.

I dip, then rise—
flit and fly.

Trust my insight.
Protect my heart.

Alone
in my circular world returning.

Air, and the glint

She Who Lives Between Worlds

Before she had wings, she had only water.

She lived beneath the surface, where everything was close and slow and known.
The current shaped her. She belonged to that world completely,
even when she did not feel at home.

She did not yet know that belonging and becoming are not the same.

She moved in circles there. Not trapped—contained.

The circle taught her patience. It taught her endurance. It taught her how to
survive, how to remain when movement was impossible, how to listen to forces
larger than herself.

Still, something in her longed. Not for escape. For air.
She did not know what air was. Only that something above her called without
sound.

For a long time, she ignored it. Survival was enough. Until survival became too
small for what she was becoming.

The change began quietly. Her body grew restless inside its certainty. The
sustaining circles began to feel like preparation. The water no longer defined her
edges. It held her, but it did not complete her.

She followed the silent call upward. Not with confidence. With instinct.
When she reached the surface, the crossing was not immediate

She lingered at the threshold suspended between what had formed her and what
had not yet claimed her.

She learned that transformation does not occur in the place you leave or the place
you arrive. It occurs in the crossing. Her body opened.

What had once allowed her only to endure began to allow her to rise.

Wings emerged—fragile, lace-like, precise. They did not appear strong. But they were exact.
Her jaw remained fierce. Softness did not replace her strength. It refined it.

She left the water, not as rejection, but as continuation.
When she entered the air, she discovered something unexpected. She was not meant to land.

On earth, she was awkward. Her body did not yet belong to stillness. Gravity did not define her. Her design was not for permanence, but for motion.

She was made for the space between. She learned to glide where others stood. She learned to dip without falling. She learned to rise without force.

The wind did not control her. It revealed her.
She glittered not for admiration, but as consequence of light meeting structure.

She lived in circles still, but they were chosen. Circles of attention. Circles of listening. Circles that connected water to sky, past to future, solitude to presence.

She did not belong to water though she remembered it.
She did not belong to earth, though she touched it.
She did not belong fully to air, though she moved within it.
She belonged to the threshold.

She became the messenger of emergence,
a breath of light passing through air—
transformation erases nothing, it carries all forward,
wing by wing,
listening for what stirs to rise.

She became the Dragonfly.
She Who Lives Between Worlds.

The Flight of Possibility

Before she understood flight,
she understood water.
She lived at its surface—
where reflection trembles
and nothing holds a single shape for
long.

The sky was not a destination.
It was a question.

She waited in the thin seam
between immersion and light—
half memory,
half horizon.

When she emerged,
It was not upward.
It was outward.

Her wings unfolded like geometry
drawn in air—
four transparent thresholds
crossed by light.

She did not rise in a single arc.
She circled.
A widening.
Then a narrowing.
Then widening again.

The world was not something to
escape.
It was something to engage
without finality.
Possibility did not live in distance.

It lived in relation—
in the subtle shift of heat,
in the tremor of wind,
in the shimmer along water's skin.

She hovered.
Not suspended—
attentive.

Each pause was a pivot.
Each pivot, a recalibration.
Each recalibration, a new
circumference.

Her circular world was not
confinement.
It was continuity.

She returned to where she had been
and found it altered.
She dipped toward the surface
and saw a different sky reflected
there.

Flight was not departure from
depth.
It was tension held
between depth and air.

She learned the art of micro-turning.
—
a fraction of tilt.
a subtle correction mid-current.
She could dart without losing
center.

Hover without dissolving.

Descend without regression.
Rise without abandonment.

Nothing was fixed.
Everything was responsive.

In her circling, she discovered
that change and creation were not
separate acts.

What shifted within her altered the
arc she traced.
What she traced altered what she
understood.

The inner and outer world did not mirror
each other.
They conversed.

Creation was not invention from
nothing.
It was response—
to heat,
to light,
to pressure,
to memory.

She did not fly to arrive.
She flew to dialogue.

Every circle revised the last.
Every descent gathered material.
Every ascent released it in new
form.

Possibility was not a door.

It was atmosphere.
She did not leave the threshold.
She inhabited it.

And the motion did not end.
It continued—
precise,
attentive,
alive.

She was not between worlds.
She was turning between them.

Psychological Translation—Emergence and Transition

The Dragonfly represents the phase of transformation where movement
becomes conscious.

After depth has been endured and boundary has taken form, life does not simply
resume.
It recalibrates.

This phase is less about defense and more about orientation.
The nervous system begins to trust adjustment.
Breath moves more freely.
Attention widens without scattering.
The body no longer prepares for
impact at every turn.
There is a space between stimulus and response.

The Dragonfly teaches micro-turning.
A slight shift in angle.
A pause mid-motion.
A willingness to circle back rather
than force forward.

Psychologically, this appears as:
Changing direction without shame.
Revisiting an idea without collapse.
Holding more than one perspective
at once.
Identity loosens.
Not in confusion—
into flexibility.

Possibility, in this phase, is not fantasy.
It is relational awareness.
The individual begins to sense that life is not a fixed path—
but a field of currents.

Heat shifts.
Wind shifts.
Internal weather shifts.
And instead of resisting those shifts,
they adjust.
Creation begins to feel less like effort
and more like response.

What changes inside alters the arc of action.
What is expressed reshapes what is understood.
The inner and outer enter dialogue.

This phase can feel unfamiliar at first.
Without vigilance to organize around,
there is openness.
Without rigid direction,
there is space.

The core tension here is subtle:
How to expand without losing center.

The Dragonfly does not abandon what has been learned in depth or shadow.
She moves with it.
Circling is not regression.
It is refinement.
Returning is not failure.
It is revision.

Emergence, in this cosmology is not arrival at a final form.
It is the capacity to remain in
motion
without losing one's axis.

The Dragonfly marks the moment when survival becomes possibility.
—and possibility becomes creative presence.
She is not between worlds.
She is the turning between them.

Turn

Nothing is final

The Lizard

Myth of Remembering

She Who Remembers the Sun

The Lizard

Lizards stare from the side.
They know time.
They shed without hesitation.

They listen
with ancient faces
and perfect nonchalance.

They rise,
catching breezes—
unafraid to stretch the neck.

They remember the sun
and remain.

She Who Remembers the Sun

Before she remembered the sun
she endured the cold.

Not dramatic cold—
but the subtle withdrawal of warmth
that keeps the body vigilant
long after danger has passed.

She learned the ground
before she trusted the sky.
She pressed herself to stone
not to disappear,
but to measure.

Heat was not indulgence.
It was information.
She did not move constantly.
She moved precisely.
While others rushed toward motion,
she waited for temperature.

Her stillness was not retreat.
It was listening.

The sun did not rescue her.
It met her.

She angled her body toward it
with ancient intelligence—
skin opening,
blood warming,
muscle softening by degrees.
Warmth did not overwhelm.
It accumulated.

Through spine.
Through belly.
Through the small hinges of her
hands.

The body that has known survival
does not abandon vigilance easily.
It recalibrates.

She allowed the heat to enter slowly,
testing its consistency.
When it held,
she lengthened.
When it faded;
she did not panic.
She adjusted.

Basking was not passivity.
It was regulation.

A pause long enough
for breath to settle
without collapsing.
A pause long enough
for the nervous system
to recognize safety
without needing to flee it.

She did not reject movement.
She conserved it.

She stretched when blood required
circulation.
She rose when direction was clear.
She rested when heat asked her to
remain.
Nothing in her was wasted.

Nothing in her was forced.
She understood that motion without
regulation
burns itself out.
She understood that stillness
without warmth
turns to stone.

She learned the rhythm between.

Sun.
Shade.
Sun again.
Pause.
Stretch.
Proceed.

The spine no longer sharpened.
The jaw no longer braced.
The breath lowered and remained.
Warmth reached the bone.

And from that warmth,
movement became sustainable.
She did not need to flee shadow.
She carried heat within her.

And because she remembered the
sun,
she could rise
without abandoning the ground.

She became the Lizard.
She Who Remembers the Sun.

Psychological Translation — Regulation and Embodiment

The Lizard marks the phase of transformation
where expansion becomes livable.

After immersion.
After boundary.
After widening.
The body must learn how to remain.

This is not dramatic work.
It is temperate work.
A system shaped by survival
does not immediately trust warmth.
It scans for interruption.
It braces for return.

Embodiment begins when
vigilance can soften without dissolving.

The Lizard teaches rhythm.
Pause long enough for breath to settle.
Move only when energy gathers.
Rest without rehearsing escape.

Regulation is not the absence of intensity.
It is the capacity to return to center after it.
The body learns that stillness is not collapse.
That warmth can stay.
That quiet does not signal danger.

In this phase strength becomes subtle.
Energy is not spent to prove aliveness.
It is conserved to sustain it.

Embodiment does not mean stagnation.
It means inhabiting one's own temperature.

Insight may open the field.
Perspective may widen it.
But the body must experience
safety again and again
before it believes the change

The Lizard reminds us that
transformation is not complete
when we understand it.
It is complete when we can live inside it.

Sun.

Shade.

Sun again.

Breath lowers.

Muscle softens.

The spine no longer anticipates

impact.

From regulated stillness movement

becomes sustainable.

And what once required vigilance

becomes simply living.

Stone keeps the memory of stars

Remain

Warmth will return

Integration

Confluence

The archetypes were never separate.
They appeared distinct so that their movements could be seen.
But it is lived experience, they interweave.

Depth does not disappear when boundary forms.
Boundary does not vanish when possibility expands.
Possibility does not dissolve when embodiment settles.
They layer.

Water remains in the blood.
Shadow remains in the spine.
Air remains in the breath.
Earth remains in the bone.

Integration is not the sequencing of elements.
It is their simultaneity.
At times, immersion is required.
At times, discernment.
At times, expansion.
At times, stillness.

Maturity is not choosing one element as identity.
It is recognizing which movement is needed
without abandoning the others.

The Mermaid teaches capacity.
The Raven teaches contour.
The Dragonfly teaches calibration.
The Lizard teaches sustainability.

Together, they form a living system.

Transformation is rarely linear.
It cycles.

Depth may return after expansion.
Boundary may sharpen after embodiment.
Stillness may follow movement.
Movement may follow stillness.

Each element leaves an imprint
that remains accessible.
The cosmology is not a ladder.
It is a rhythm.

When movement becomes dominant,
imbalance appears.
When all movement is accessible,
coherence emerges.

Integration is not a final state.
It is responsiveness across conditions.

The body holds this naturally.
Breath deepens and narrows.
Muscle contracts and releases.
Attention expands and focuses.
The elements do the same.

To live within this cosmology
 is to recognize its phases
and move through them
without fragmentation.

The elemental family is a map of lived process.
And when the movements are understood as one system,
identity no longer fractures under change.
It adapts.

The Shared Ascent

She did not rise alone.
She was shaped by depth
before she understood breath.
She was steadied by shadow
before she trusted her own outline.
She was widened by air
before she knew she could turn.
She was warmed by earth
before she believed she could remain.

Each came when needed.
None remained separate
The one who endured deepened
her capacity.
The one who discerned clarified
her contour.
The one who widened opened
her range.
The one who steadied grounded
her remaining.

They did not compete within her.
They composed her.

When she sinks,
she remembers depth.

When she sharpens
she remembers truth.

When she turns,
she remembers possibility.

When she settles,
she remembers warmth.

Rising was never upward.
It was coming into relation.

A quiet symmetry emerged—
when to soften,
when to define,
when to widen,
when to remain.

Heart open.
Will clarified.
Awareness spacious.
Body steady.

The four did not lift her above the world.
They returned her to it.

Water.

Shadow.

Air.

Earth.

Soften.
Define.
Widen.
Settle.

Sink.
See.
Turn.
Remain.

Not upward.
Within.

Again.

Here

Return

Return

She does not feel different.
She feels uninterrupted.

The water no longer pulls her beneath perception.
The shadow no longer asks to be named.
The wing does not circle.
The stone does not brace.

They are present—
but they do not intrude.

Morning arrives without symbolism.
Light moves across the floor without instruction.
The body stands without asking if it deserves to.

Breath enters.
Breath leaves.

Nothing is conquered.
Nothing is transcended.

There is no final ascent.
There is only inhabiting.

She does not return to who she was.
She returns to where she is.

The elements remain.
That is enough

Becoming exhaled into being